ROSICRUCIAN KABBALAH:
THE KINGDOM OF GOD

By Alber Jhouney
(Albert Jounet)
1887

Originally published as "Le Royaume de Dieu".
Translated by Alex Bushman 2019

Table of Contents

Translator's Foreword

Albert Jounet (1863-1923) was a French mystic and Kabbalist who wrote under the nom de plume "Alber Jhouney". He and Rene Caillie founded the Fraternite de l'Etoile in 1889 and published a monthly review called L'Etoile from 1889 to 1895. Jounet's fraternity, monthly periodical and numerous writings were primarily dedicated to the esoteric Christian Kabbalah. In the writings of L'Etoile he referred to this as Messianic Kabbalah.

This book was originally published in 1887 under the title "Le Royaume de Dieu" (The Kingdom of God). The famed Rosicrucian Stanislas De Guaita included an excerpt of this work in his book "At the Threshold of Mystery" and an excerpt was also included in the famous esoteric periodical "L'Initiation".

According to Stanislas de Guaita –

"The book Le Royaume de Dieu (The Kingdom of God) encloses, in less than a hundred pages, all the theological and dogmatic substance of Kabbalah. It was by an operation of marvelous alchemy that Mr. Alber Jhouney was able to condense, while elucidating the form and the very substance, what Rabelais would have called "the substantive marrow" of the Zohar."

"...here is the book which one must read to initiate oneself into the mysteries of the Zohar."

Given Albert Jounet's influence on Stanislas de Guaita and his involvement in the French Rose-Croix movement of "La Belle Epoque", I have decided to slightly rename this translation. This then leads us to ask the question, what is Rosicrucian Kabbalah?

Stanislas de Guaita, the founder of the Ordre Kabbalistique Rose Croix, provides us with some insight into that question:

"The Zohar has married the Gospel; the spirit has fertilized the soul; and immortal works have been the fruits of this union. Kabbalah, having become Catholic in the school of Saint John, the master of the masters, incarnates in an admirable metaphysical form (and not a bastard, as some brains have judged it) the absolute Spirit of the science of justice and love, which vivifies internally the dead letter of all orthodoxies."

This short yet potent work takes us on a journey through the Kabbalist's Etz Chaim, the Tree of Life. Each chapter explores the alchemical essence of the 10 sephiroth that compose the tree of life.

With this we gain some insight into the nature of God, Truth, and Man.

Albert Jounet's works are largely unknown and untranslated outside of the Francophone circles. I have added notations when necessary to clarify certain points of linguistic or esoteric interest. My notations are marked as "A.B." to differentiate those from the notations in the original text. I have done my best to provide the essence of what Albert was communicating as opposed to strict transliteration. That being said, any and all mistakes are my own.

Thank you for joining me in this adventure down the Tree of Life.

For more of my translations and other works, go to thealexbushman.blogspot.com

Sincerely,

-Alex Bushman

(Cover art from Albert Jounet's monthly periodical L'Etoile)

GOD

KETHER

I.   The Creator and Man

1.   The Eternal said: I am in Humanity as humanity is in the world: All thoughts of man I think, in their totality, and his feelings live in me.

2.   Kether, by Tiphereth, impregnates Malkuth.   The Ancient of Days, by the King, possesses the Bride.

3.   I am man - and that which is most intimate in him, as blood is united to the heart, as the perfume of the lily is the lily itself.

4.   Yet the created Spirits, men and angels, are real beings; their freedom remains as indestructible as me.

5.   I am the occult and infinite Sun from which the stars spring. I am the Love where Souls burn like the stars in the Aour.

6.   True love is the voluntary, conscious, unselfish gift of the whole being, the exaltation of the Spirit to the eternal sacrifice.

7.   I wanted that there were beings separate from me, and that for their salvation - and their future happiness is my Heaven.

8.   Profound happiness can only be embraced by the grip of absolute Charity, Truth, Grace, and Justice – the possession of God.

9.   To possess all my being is to become me: The happiness of creatures is accomplished by the willful and infinite gift of themselves to God and to other creatures - for the heart of God is Love.

10.   But if Souls remained bound to me by my will and not by theirs, if they were not free to love or to hate, they could not truly love.

11.   One does not give if one is not master of refusing.

12.   It is better for creatures to hate me than to passively obey me.

13.   To hate me is to be able to love me.

14. I am perfect by my very nature: The Soul choosing the Good by its will is created perfect: Freedom is the divinity of the Soul.

15. Abyss between the Creator and the creatures, I am my own cause by me, they become their own cause by me.

16. Rigorous Justice controls the world, it is the world. Its organs, its aptitudes, its environment.

17. The universal analogy, incarnation of Justice, groups the stars and, on the stars group beings, distributes matter in zones.

18. The invisible stars follow the Law of the visible stars.

19. The development of your intelligence and your heart can only evolve according to this Law of analogy and Justice.

20. If you do not work patiently to create in your soul the spiritual organs that touch and contemplate me,

21. You will always ignore me.

22. Without this inner creation, praying to me is useless: I will not contradict myself, I will not violate the order that I desired.

23.   So you see, if you worry about your imperfection, how far you are from knowing me by science.

24.   Do you deny me because I remain inaccessible to you?

25.   Your soul, emanating from me, keeps an obscure awareness of this Principle of its being, which is one of my thoughts, and by this thought, of my infinity.

26.   This awareness of what is at once beyond you, in your depth, and above you, in your dreams, is Faith.

27.   If you want to express your faith, it escapes you enough for your dogmas to be perishable, but not so completely that they are empty.

28.   You, however, have the duty of seeking to express your faith, for rest will be given to you only at the farthest heights of my abyss, and this search begins your ascent into my abyss.

29.   If you believe in my Unity, what can your beliefs be?

30.   That I am everything, that there is no creation, and that the beings, outside me, are appearances.

31.   That I am everything because I have created everything and that the beings are real.

32.   If the second belief is yours, you see, that if true, my love and my omnipotence have more reality than in the first [belief] by giving me the strength to perform even outside of me. By this I am all beings for the second as for the first belief.

33.   There are proofs which incline you to the second faith, but in the state of your body and of your thought before you are regenerated they have not the evidence and cannot be imposed by certainty.

34.   Your heart must choose: Decisive ordeal. When you have undergone it, I know if the generosity of your soul has passed the proofs to persevere in its ideal.

35.   Because in the first belief there is no freedom for you; for me there is no love.

36.   Do not be discouraged by the baseness of reason and the uncertain exaltation of faith.

37.   You have in you the discernment of Good and Evil.

38.   When you deceive yourself in your first acts, if your will is good, you will discover little by little the moral Law.

39.   Know that science does not reach me, that vision cannot guess me.

40.   You will understand me if you are just.

II.   The Sephiroth

1.   Woe, said the Zohar, to him whom does not see, in the Law, but stories and words like the others.

2.   Could one not, thanks to the doctors of the Earth, compose a law more pompous than Scripture?

3.   In the Book, every word is a Mystery.

4.   The Commandments are the body of the Law. The stories, the clothes of the body. But the Law has a soul.

5.   The inner sense of the Word teaches the Magus that God manifested by ten Sephiroth: God, says the Zohar, is like a sea.

6.   From this sea springs a stream towards the earth which is called Wisdom, this stream then falls and opens as a lake in a basin called Intelligence.

7.   From this basin, like seven channels, emerge the seven other Sephiroth: Mercy, Justice, Beauty, Triumph, Glory, Foundation, Kingdom.

8. The infinite Being has no name. It is not the beings gathered in an abyss, nor the unity of blessings descending upon us from its depths.

9. Indefinable, Incomprehensible.

10. Non being for who wants to conceive it, absolute reality in itself.

11. The Word, written by correspondence, is not understood by the profane up to the inner meaning.

12. Yet the inner meaning remains in the Word that the profane read and the apparent meaning, which for them is very different from the occult Truth whose presence they ignore, is closely united to it and appears as its visible emanation for the Sages who penetrate the triple Mysteries of the Law: In the same way, God is manifest in the Sephiroth.

13. For the created Intelligences, which always remain profane before the uncreated Intelligence, only the Sephiroth are visible and for them very different from YHVH.

14. But, for God, the Sephiroth or the attributes which radiate it are united to his essence and form an extension of it.

15.   There are three worlds: The divine world, the intellectual world and the natural world.

16.   The last Sephiroth, Malkuth, is the Kingship of the Sephiroth over the astral light and the universal matter and not a distinct Emanation.

17.   The Tower of the Sephiroth is reflected in the starry ether.

18.   The reflection moves and dominates the ether, and this domination is called Malkuth.

19.   The first Triad, that of the divine world, comprises the metaphysical attributes.

20.   The second Triad, that of the intellectual world, comprises the moral attributes.

21.   The third Triad, that of the natural world, comprises the generative attributes.

22.   The first Triad contains: Kether, the Crown, Chokmah, Wisdom, and Binah, Intelligence.

23.   The second Chesed, Grace, Gevurah, Justice, Tiphereth, Beauty.

24.   The third, Netzach, Triumph, Hod, Glory, Yesod, Generation.

25.   Kether expresses the absolute Being, not the Absolute itself, God, which remains incomprehensible, but the highest, the most one, the most profound conception that the thought forms of the Substance.

26.   Chokmah is the male Spirit, Wisdom, the power of expansion through which creation operates, the Logos.

27.   Binah is the female Spirit, the form that Love fertilizes, the restrictive power that tightens and contains the Spirit of Wisdom and prevents it from dispersing vainly.

28.   Chesed expresses Grace, Mercy, it is also called magnificence, for mercy is born of the generosity of the soul; it is the male and active principle of morality. To devote oneself to all and to give oneself entirely.

29.   Geburah is Severity, the feminine principle of morality; to concentrate, to seek purity by the distancing from and contempt of evil.

30.   Tiphereth, Beauty, balances in it Purity and Splendor.

31.   Netzach is the multiplication of Beings, the development of Infinity, the male principle of force.

32.   Hod, Glory, expresses the stability of forms, the fixation of the fertilizing power, the feminine Principle of the creative force.

33.   Yesod, Generation, the balanced result of Netzach and Hod, is the base of the Sephiroth and the Foundation of Being.

34.   Malkuth reflects the nine upper Sephiroth. Like the sea where, down on the horizon, the vast Orion with its nine dazzling stars is reflected.

35.   The divine world: The Spirit. The intellectual world: The Law. The natural world: The Force.

36.   The divine world is the unlimited free thought, the absolute Truth created by Wisdom and contemplated in Intelligence, and the exclusive Unity in which reaches out, exalted one by the other, the two great powers of the Soul.

37.   The divine world is, in the Correspondences, Religion, Metaphysics, Prophetic and Contemplative Poetry, Sacred Architecture and Music.

38.   To love God without measure, to never descend from ecstasy knowing the consequences, never to sacrifice the Ideal

to its incomplete realization, seal of the Elect (Élus), destiny of the Prophet-Kings.

39.   The intellectual world regulates, restricts, analyzes, compares; it exercises thought in all that is logical, mathematical, symmetrical, limited.

40.   The Binary governs it as Unity [governs] the divine world. Man discovers how he must act in all that can be governed by a law. Here Man discovers how he must act in all that can be governed by a Law.

41.   The divine world has no law. Here to love God with a pure and infinite love animates everything.

42.   But one does not penetrate this light without obeying all the prescriptions of the intellectual world.

43.   To become the true image of God as we can understand it, we must contain, like him, the ten Sephiroth and balance them.

44.   But the Balance has to be according to the order.

45.   And the upper Sephiroth rule the inferiors by the middle.

46.   Correspondances of the intellectual world: Morality, science, legislation, profane arts.

47.   The natural world begets, destroys and renews. In man, it corresponds to instincts, to appetites; in creation, to fatal forces; in primitive numbers, to the Ternary.

48.   Analogies of the natural world: The sexual embrace, war, the land with its deserts and its luxuriance, the ocean with its storms and its regular tide, the people, the voice of the crowds ...

49.   The Divine World: The Ideal. The Intellectual World: Duty. The Natural World: Passion.

50.   Thus the image of God and universal Harmony are constituted by the Balance of three Spheres, each of which contains three Principles balanced between them.

51.   The Central column of the Sephiroth: Kether, Tiphereth, Yesod, Malkuth.

52.   Ten equals seven: The decade includes four Unities and three Binaries.

53.   The four Unities are the four central Sephiroth and the three Binaries are: Chokmah-Binah, Chesed-Gevurah, Netzach-Hod.

54. And this is a great Mystery.

55. Kether is the Ancient of Days, Tiphereth the King, Malkuth the Queen.

56. The radiance of Kether falls on the King who communicates it to the Queen:

57. God by Humanity sows the Nature of thoughts.

58. The love of the Queen rises to the King who brings back to Kether the Soul of the Queen:

59. Nature, by Humanity, brings back to God the fallen Souls.

60. The Sephiroth correspond to the members of the Man: When I created Adam Kadmon, said the Eternal, my spirit gushed forth from his body like an immense flash that shone at once on the waves of the seven million heavens, and my ten splendors were his members.

61. Kether, my will, my being, was his forehead, Wisdom and Intelligence his shoulders, Magnificence his right arm and Justice his left arm, Beauty his heart, his thighs Triumph and Glory; by Yesod, he fertilized the primitive Heva, and his whole body was the Kingdom of God.

III. The Trinity

1. The Father, the Son, the Spirit.

2. In the Lord himself, beyond the Sephiroth that represent him, in the Incomprehensible, ecstasy glimpses the Holy Trinity, whose manifested Triads, spiritual and material, embody[1] the Image.

3. Qui scrutator est majestatis opprimetur a gloria[2].

4. He who alters a symbol, even when he does not know its meaning, damages the meaning and destroys the harmony of heaven and earth.

5. There is darkness that is better than the light of man because this darkness gives life and this light causes death.

6. If you declare: I believe in the reality of God and I reject the Trinity, you contradict yourself. There is no reality without Ternary; in God, which is Unity, the Ternary is the Trinity.

---

[1] A.B.: incarnate
[2] A.B.: Proverbs 25:27; "whoever is an investigator of what is majestic will be overwhelmed by glory."

7.   If you want to think a living and not abstract thought and if you reject the Trinity you will only be able to reject two of the three people and worship only one of them, for God is conceivable for living contemplation only in the form of these persons.

8.   But then you will see, if you reject two people, that you degrade God and that you reduce the tree of life to the roots, the trunk, leaves and flowers.

9.   If you accept the three persons and deny that God is equally in his fullness in each one of them you degrade God because empty forms are not a development.

10.   God is an absolute Unity. He is thus contained entirely in each of the forms of his development or these forms would be apart from him.

11.   But the People constitute one sole Being. Their isolation would break Unity as much as their inequality.

12.   Souls, praying in one of the highest circles of paradise, desired a vision to express to them the intelligence of the mystery of the Holy Trinity.

13.   They then saw, in a black sky without stars, and higher than all the starry skies, the summit of a mountain

whose base plunged below the hells and whose flanks rose through all the circles of the immense ether.

14. From this summit fell a spring which formed a river, and the river bathed the universe; it snaked through all the levels of the night, rushing and frothing from one to the other, and carried stars in its waters.

15. A splendor emanated from both the river and the mountain, and penetrated both.

16. Then an archangel said to those who wanted to understand the mystery:

17. The mountain cannot flow through worlds like the river, and the river cannot remain motionless at the center of the worlds like the mountain.

18. Without the splendor which unites them, the mountain would ignore the magnificent sweetness and charity of the river; the river would forget, while nourishing the worlds, the solitude and the purity of the mountain.

19. Contemplate the perfect Being: must he not, like the mountain, remain immutable and solitary; like the river, to vivify creation; like the splendor, to unite between them the Word and the Absolute?

20.   If he were wholly in one of these powers, he would not enjoy the fullness of others.

21.   If he did not remain one, he would become three finite gods, each incapable of the will of the other two.

22.   God is ONE because He is infinite. He is TRIPLE because he is unlimited.

CHOKMAH

I.   <u>Salvation</u>

1.   Et verbum caro factum est[3]. The Mystery of the Incarnation and the Mystery of the Redemption, salvation of the Humanity, divine image of the works by which the spirit is regenerated.

2.   Separate grace and will, salvation becomes impossible.

3.   Without grace, the will would have no heaven to conquer. Without the effort of the will, grace would not save man because the resurrection of the soul is the effort towards God.

4.   The Incarnation and the Redemption, the supreme charity of grace.

5.   The Incarnation and the Redemption, the ideal of the trials and victories of the will.

6.   God descended to become flesh, and by his descent, rose to become sorrowful flesh.

---

[3] And the Word was made flesh.

7.   Contemplate this Mystery in your hours of despair. May your agony itself even be useful to men.

8.   The suffering of Golgotha and the Garden of Olives saved men, and God was thirsty for it.

9.   By the Incarnation Man-God was born. The two natures were merged into one; purity and beauty were alive, and life was sanctified.

10.   The highest Ideal has all its grandeur and all its grace only after having undergone the trials of the earth. The sky, shining with stars, moves less than the earth where, in the human breasts, burn ardent pains.

11.   No human ideal is as profound as the splendor of God, but human suffering is as profound.

12.   God made himself man to give us the majesty of his glory and to cover the majesty of despair and death.

13.   Unite the purity of your repentance to the purity of God.

II.   <u>Love and Selfishness</u>[4]

1.   Love, voluntary and conscious, is all virtue; selfishness, voluntary and conscious, is the radical and intimate vice, the irreducible principle of evil.

2.   Good consists in perfection, the principle of perfection is the will to be perfect, to want to be perfect, it is to prefer the Ideal over one's own satisfaction, it is to love the Ideal.

3.   It is to create it in oneself and in others.

4.   When we truly love we act in accordance with what we love.

5.   Devotion to perfection affirms that it is the sovereign Good and gives birth to Faith.

6.   The effort to create perfection in oneself affirms that salvation is possible and gives birth to Hope.

7.   The sacrifice, not of his own moral perfection(to defile one's soul for another would be to sacrifice God to

---

[4] A.B.: Égoïsme can be translated as egoism or selfishness and as such either term can be used interchangeably in this book.

another and not oneself), but of his whole being to the salvation of others, asserts that the life of perfection is sacrifice and gives birth to Charity.

8.   The three sublime virtues are completed by the four practical virtues: Justice, Prudence, Strength[5], Temperance. In its totality, Justice is the resolution to always act as God would act.

9.   In principle, Prudence is the knowledge of God and of his will.

10.   Prudence balances justice and prevents it from going astray by giving the resolution of righteousness the just rule.

11.   In its totality, Strength is heroism and constancy to remain just in temptation and martyrdom.

12.   Far from this virtue commanding the Élus[6] to conquer power by material means, his help confirms them in the contempt of these ways.

13.   True Strength consists not in dominating the people for a time, but to possess eternity by renunciation; when the Messiah will rule the people, his kingship will be divine,

---

[5] A.B.: in French "Force" can be translated as force, power, strength, might, etc.
[6] A.B.: elect

because after having ascended to his Father by the Passion, he will only find in the Kingdom, the Almighty, a duty of charity and not a conquest.

14. In principle Temperance is the science of temptations.

15. The discernment which recognizes in each work met and in happiness offered, if this work or this happiness, however noble they may appear, comes from God, and if to seduce us, Satan did not take the form of Jesus Christ.

16. Temperance balances and counsels Strength as Prudence [balances and counsels] Justice. Two heroic virtues and two pensive virtues.

17. The four cardinal virtues are the development of Justice, which itself is only the practice of Charity, a practice that leads to the realization of Hope and Faith.

18. The source of the three sublime virtues is an impulse of the Soul out of itself.

19. It is the devotion to God and neighbor which is the condition for personal holiness.

20. If devotion to God stopped for a man to raise his intelligence and his heart without thinking of others,

21.   It will be judged that this man is an egoist because his love for perfection does not prevail to generosity. This love was therefore self-interested and cold at its origin.

22.   You will judge the trees by their fruits and men by their abnegation[7].

23.   Sacrifice consumes liberty, since through it it exalts itself until it delivers itself from its attachments to free being, inspires the purest passion of the Ideal, since through it one seeks to create the Ideal but in another.

24.   Sacrifice is above all a miraculous grace, a virtue which has no cause, being the cause of all the others. It resembles God: God is sacrifice.

25.   For the sacrifice to be meritorious, it must be voluntary and conscious. The acts of a being belong to him only if he intends them.

26.   Martyrdom sought by folly and intoxication is without merit.

27.   Egoism is the opposite of sacrifice, not hatred. Hatred can be selfless.

---

[7] A.B.: abnegation – the act of renouncing or rejecting something; self-denial

28.   Selfishness chains freedom and makes the Soul slave to its interest; it degrades the love of the Ideal to make the Ideal an instrument and an industry.

29.   But like sacrifice, it offers a primitive and irreducible character.

30.   Egoism[8] finds the sovereign Good not in submission to the Eternal[9], but in the satisfaction of the creature, it affirms the creature superior to God and gives birth to pride.

31.   Selfishness disdains to regenerate itself because it thinks only of satisfying itself and giving birth to idleness.

32.   It exploits others for its pleasure, far from devoting itself to ennobling them, and gives birth to lust.

33.   The spirit of lust, not only to the excesses of the flesh, but to all the sensualities, to all the appetites, to all the iniquitous exploitations, is intoxicated and transformed into voracity.

34.   Lust and greed are awakened and overexcited by envy.

35.   Iniquitous desire destroys what resists it by violence.

---

[8] A.B.: selfishness
[9] A.B.: in French, the term Eternel can be translated as "Lord"

36.   And what it delights it keeps jealously for itself, by greed.

37.   The Dragon, egoism, shakes its seven heads and roars pride against Faith, idleness against Hope, lust against Charity, greed against Justice, envy against Prudence, violence against Strength, and avarice against Temperance.[10]

III.   The Commandments

1.   Non habebis Deos alienos coram me.

2.   Non assumes nomen Dei Domini tui in vanum.

3.   Memento ut siem Sabbati sanctifices.

4.   Honora patrem tuum et matrem tuam.

5.   Non occides.

6.   Non machaberis.

7.   Non furtum facies.

---

[10] Here we have a version of the seven deadly sins and seven virtues

8.   Non loqueris contra proximum tuum falsum testimonium.

9.   Non concupisces domum proximi tui.

10.   Nec desiderabis uxorem ejus, non servum, non ancillam, non bovem, non asinum, nec omnia quae illius sunt.

11.   The first three commandments: Divine world.

12.   The three following: Moral world.

13.   The last four: Natural world.

14.   The first corresponds to Kether, the second to Chokmah, the third to Binah.

15.   The fourth to Chesed, the fifth to Geburah, the sixth to Tiphereth

16.   The seventh to Netzach, the eigth to Hod, the ninth to Yesod, and the tenth to Malkuth.

17.   God is Unity, the Absolute, the pure Spirit and the Mystery. You will not worship multiple gods, neither creatures nor anything known, material, human, angelic, of creation.

18.   God is wisdom, love in justice and generosity. You will not mix his name or religion with anything false, personal, sterile, mortal or transitory.

19.   The wisdom of God is in the form of Intelligence; religion is in the form of worship; you will not neglect the sacred ceremonies of the seventh day because the destruction of the form injures the spirit and that which ceases to be realized becomes powerless and null.

20.   You shall remember that nothing is without roots; and you will respect your ancestors. You will not blaspheme the work of centuries.

21.   You will not strike your neighbor with any cruelty or hatred. I have reserved vengeance, says the Lord.

22.   You will not degrade your neighbor nor yourself with lust. Lust is murder by degradation. And there are murderers who find lust in death.

23.   You will not steal because triumph without loyalty will be judged vile. To steal is to win without working. Gain without work, victory without loyalty.

24.   You will not bear false witness because nothing is stable but truth. This truth that you have distorted will be in judgment the condemnation and the hell of your lie.

25.   You will not covet the property of your neighbor because the foundation of nations like spheres is fruitfulness according to order and goodness. Order is destroyed when the fruits of labor are not assured to the one who has made them grow.

26.   You will not covet your neighbor's wife, his servant, or anything your neighbor possesses. The kingdom of the righteous subsists by fidelity.

27.   The first commandment affirms the unity of the Elohim and its Trinity.

28.   The second obliges us not to desecrate speech nor spiritual songs.

29.   The third [obliges us] to be regenerated by the inner worship.

30.   The fourth to venerate the Church, to worship the commandments of God.

31.   The fifth not to kill souls by making them ungodly.

32.   The sixth not to distort the Word and not to invent heresies.

33.   The seventh not to deceive, not to deprive thy neighbor of the truth.

34.   The eighth not to declare that error is truth.

35.   The ninth not to covet the spiritual merit of thy neighbor, to try not to occupy yourself with his virtue or his science.

36.   By the tenth a defense is pronounced analogous to that which the ninth pronounces but with details which will be exposed in the book of Divine Science.

BINAH

I.   Religion

1.   Religion, development both natural and divine of the Word in Humanity.

2.   The evolution of Humanity and the earth takes place according to two laws.

3.   The first results in a motion analogous to the growth and decay of a tree, an animal, a man, during the seasons, the rise and fall of empires.

4.   A vast motion offering an immensity of exaltation and general decadence, during which a multitude of exaltations and partial decadences rise and fall.

5.   So that, during the great exaltation which has not yet been completed, several decadences have fallen, and that during the great decadence several eras of glory will rise to their apogee.

6.   The science of this law, in its most extensive and subtle applications, confirms to the Prophets and the Magi their inspirations.

7.   And by it is certain the future reign of Yodhéva in the world.

8.   The second law does not regulate the cycles of time. It proceeds the same eternally.

9.   It is the Law of Hierarchy that makes certain men the material or spiritual Kings of men and of certain Ideas the ruler of others.

10.   Religion embraces sovereign Ideas[11].

11.   Dogmas are, in the intellectual order, the Kings of Kings and the Lords of Lords.

12.   But the Law of Hierarchy classifies the dogmas themselves, and among the beliefs of an era, only one is elected.

13.   Which will kill the others.

14.   The Law of Hierarchy combines with the Law of Cycles. The higher spirits, the religions, the higher sciences, form, through time, families whose absolute exterior magnificence will burst forth only at the apogee of the great exaltation.

---

[11] A.B.: Idées in French can also mean thought, thinking, concept, etc.

15.   But the law of Hierarchy contradicts and braves the Law of Cycles in that genius is equal to genius in all times and truth to truth. Only in the dark ages genius is symbolic, truth is hidden.

16.   In the conquering centuries the word becomes more direct and science is open.

17.   As the genius among men, the solar man, as the sun among the planets, there is and always will be a solar religion in the world.

18.   This religion has slowly risen from the midnight of bestiality to the starry shadow of prophecies and symbols that the primitive Orientals and the Hebrews have contemplated in prayer.

19.   Its dawn and bloody aurora shone in the parables of Jesus and the blood of Christ and the martyrs.

20.   Its full noon will come and its royal triumph by the second advent of the Messiah.

21.   Then it will descend in the darkness as in the earth.

22.   It will be extinguished by the last of men, fallen in the ignorance of childhood by the weakness of their decrepitude and they will perish in the night.

23. But it will be reignited in eternity. Its dogmas are the meditation of God, its charity is the heart of God.

II.   <u>**Messianic Prayer**</u>

1.   Our Father who descended on the earth among us.

2.   Your name is holy and glorious in all souls.

3.   Your Kingdom has arrived.

4.   Your will is done on Earth as it is in Heaven.

5.   Give us for eternity, life and eternal truth.

6.   In all the light of Initiation we are before you only darkness.

7.   Forgive us our weakness and our offenses. We have forgiven our enemies.

8.   For are not you infinite forgiveness?

9.   What distances us from you is not your justice, but your purity.

10.   Defend us against temptation. It becomes more profound when man rises.

11.   Give us the strength to overcome evil through you.

12.   Charge us with the miseries of our brothers and give them our reward. Hosannah.

III. Messianic Symbol

1. I believe and I know, my God, that you are one.

2. Silent Father of souls and worlds you have created Spirit and matter, Earth and Heaven.

3. We see that you are realizing your works with reality and we know by the holy Kabbalah we see through the inner eyes what other creation you have prolonged in the mystery.

4. Glorious Son, incarnate Messiah you reign over the earth and the Empire of the stars.

5. Your blood streams eternally from the heavens and falls to the bottom of the abyss.

6. It is united with the universal life, it beats in all the stars and in the heart of all the living.

7. And the blasphemous mouth has in his lips your blood mingled with his, the hand that kills has in his flesh your blood mingled with his.

8. And your blood flows in the heart of Satan.

9.   A day will come when the heat of your blood has changed blasphemies into lilies, murderers into children and the heart of Satan into a heart of righteousness.

10.   Then Heaven will spill into the abyss and the abyss will vanish into Heaven.

11.   Holy Spirit, through the Ternary and the Quaternary, you beget and renew every Law, you who have given Symbols and Numbers to masters of the Light.

12.   And you have gathered all men in the one Church, the bride of the Messiah, Initiated into the mysteries of the God of the Magi.

13.   The Prophets, Martyrs, Apostles, Saints, Virgins, Righteous, dead and alive, are one in your infinite love.

14.   You hand over their sins to those who have loved.

15.   You discourage the evil by returning to him the consciousness of his nothingness, at the height of his pride.

16.   The Elus[12] are resurrected in glory and one day the universal being will be resurrected in glory, for eternal ecstasy and eternal life. Alleluia

---

[12] A.B.: Elect

TRUTH

CHESED

I.   The Grand Arcanum and Hierarchy

1.   Verum, sine mendacio, certum et verissimum. Quod superius est sicut quod est inferius et quod est inferius est sicut quod est superius ad operanda miracula rei unius.[13]

2.   All the science of the Magi is contained in the Grand Arcanum.

3.   This Axiom is revealed in an infinite number of Pantacles, symbols, legends. It is concentrated[14] for the initiate in a single word, YODHEVAVHE [יהוה], and even in a single letter, ALEPH [א].

4.   The Arcanum is manifested by the Ternary and the Quaternary, but it is neither the Ternary nor the Quaternary, it is the law of their formation.

5.   The Wisdom of the Hierophant proclaims that the universal being was created, developed and subsisted by balanced Movement.

---

[13] A.B.: This is the first section in Latin of the Emerald Tablet
[14] A.B.: summarized

6.　　The general possibility is limited. Thus there are three dimensions and six perpendicular directions.

7.　　Thus beings offer an analogy because the general properties of being are not innumerable.

8.　　The balance of the causes realized in proportional effect, is the world.

9.　　The analogies form vast groups which are subdivided by the same principle which has formed them.

10.　　This principle is the union of relative opposites and the discord of absolute opposites.

11.　　Two groups of forces, one of which is such that the whole group is animated by a single will or a single current, the other in the grip of conflicting wills and divergent currents.

12.　　The Word has seven stars in the right hand.

13.　　The Red Dragon has seven heads and ten horns.

14.　　But if, in the first group, wills or forces obey the One, it must not be that the obedience reduces them to nothing.

15. Subjected, the more their particular power will be deep, the better the group and the One will triumph.

16. They must be harmonized with each other because if, obedient to the One, they collide with each other, the power of the group will be diminished.

17. So that they do not collide, each is ranked, according to analogy and Justice, to the place that its nature merits.

18. Each has its predestined place if they are different. If they are identical they must still be ordered, but in relation to unity, assembling them in such a way as to make their direction by the One the easiest and the most certain.

19. All lasting victory is that of these axioms, and solid progress is accomplished by their invincible linking.

20. Anarchy: Powerlessness by the equality of opposing tendencies that mutually neutralize each other.

21. Decomposition: Anarchy of the cells after the disappearance of the Soul. Madness, revolt of ideas, fear and passion, culpable revolutions of instincts and feelings.

22. The order in submission to Unity, is Hierarchy.

II.   Numbers

1.   Of all the general modes of thought, number is the most abstract.

2.   It expresses the Idea of one or more beings without anything being indicated by it of their nature.

3.   But unity or multiplicity and, in multiplicity, the various Numbers are nevertheless the sign of physical properties, of moral characters.

4.   Because, for one who knows the substance internally, whether a being is one or multiple and of such particular multiplicity, does not offer itself as if by chance.

5.   The causes which maintain a being absolutely one or divide it relatively according to such or such number have a capital power.

6.   That of controlling everything in the being or of persevering the independent essential forces that compose it.

7.   So Numbers, when one knows the substance, give the eternal science, and when one ignores the substance, they give nothing.

8.   One, two, three, four Masters and principles of the sacred Numbers.

9.   One is being, two is the couple, three is the generation, four is the birth.

10.   One, two, three, four, put together give ten. The decade is the sum of the causes.

11.   Quaternary Pyramid: Yod, He, Vav, He.

12.   The Ancient of Days, the Mother, the King, the Queen.

13.   The Father, the Son, The Spirit, the Church.

14.   The Trinity, the Incarnation, the Redemption, the Kingdom of God.

15.   Being, science, experience, certainty.

16.   Thinking, reasoning, understanding, evidence.

17.   Conception, rule, beauty, work.

18.   Matter, industry, exchange, wealth.

19.   Strength, antagonism, movement, series.

20.   Law, number, analogy, groups.

21. Instinct, environment, evolution, forms.

22. Space, variety, change, time.

23. There is a host of other Quaternaries that will be listed in the Book of Divine Science.

24. To divine the future by the firmament, to penetrate the thoughts by the face, to find on the human forehead the seal of the stars which influence them, to order all of spiritual and material creation in constellations: true, all - powerful Astrology.

25. Divination is a synthetic vision of the causes in their effects and evolutions in their seeds.

26. Numbers of divination: Three, Four, Seven, Twelve.

27. The three Worlds, the four cardinal points, the four seasons, the four Elements, the seven astrological planets, the Zodiac.

28. Find out which World a being belongs to, if it is Eastern, Western, Southern, Northern, what is its element, its season, the planets that dominate it and the signs of the Zodiac.

29.   But discover especially if it is of the Light, Darkness or twilight.

30.   The principles of divination are very simple, their application very delicate. The essence of the beings which determines to what end they will serve the general forces which are recognized to them is often manifested by imperceptible movements or nuances of form and color, and, if it is a question of men, by a single sincere look among thousands.

31.   In the heavens and the light of glory, the impure is tortured by the light and concedes its anguish.

32.   It cannot hide its horror or the torments it suffers to breath: Before a demon, do you hesitate and doubt if it is not an Angel? Take it with you in the splendor of Heaven.

III. <u>Souls</u>

1.   Atziluth, Briah, Yetzirah and Assiah, the four successive spheres in which the emanation descends, each contain four worlds.

2.   There is therefore an Atziluthic Atziluth, Briah, Yetzirah and Assiah, and thus other spheres.

3.   Atziluth is the purest and Assiah the grossest of circles where the emanation of God descends.

4.   The sixteen worlds form a continuous chain, so that Atziluth is the root of Briah, Briah of Yetzirah, and Yetzirah of Assiah.

5.   Souls are created in the sphere of Atziluth. They hover there like clouds in the dawn, floating like free contemplation, innocent.

6.   But innocence is to virtue what hope is to victory.

7.   God tests souls to make them worthy of Him and of their freedom.

8.   So they cross all the worlds successively until they fall to the lowest degree of Assiah.

9. Some are weighed down by sin and forgetfulness of God; others are sent to the lower circles by the Lord, who wishes to subject them to the test, like the gold of the mines to the fire which we wish to render supremely brilliant and pure.

10. All descend and Heaven is for them only a memory and rather the memory of an Ideal than of a homeland.

11. They go down to know ignorance, hunger, remorse, slavery.

12. Flesh, despair, hatred and death.

13. And even egoism and degradation.

14. But in the material world, surrounded by selfishness and degradation as it is by its body.

15. Distraught by hunger, corrupted by the flesh, discouraged by remorse, crushed by slavery, tempted by despair and hatred.

16. If the soul, despite the ignorance which shows him only the unknown after death, and nothingness for the senses.

17.   And that leaves no existence to the Ideal beyond the dream.

18.   If the soul, alone, without God and without reason, chooses the love of men and the desire of God.

19.   The choice makes it truly noble and it begins to ascend back to Heaven.

20.   Then, in endless trials, through innumerable births, it is given the opportunity to reconquer one by one its virginity and magnificence.

21.   Until the day when the Lord says to him: I created you and you, by bloody efforts and doubts and crimes, you created me in you.

22.   And now you will possess me completely.

23.   Justice and analogy adapt and reciprocally proportion the being to the environments.

24.   The soul, immersed in the body, knows the world only by the body, it only distinctly perceives the material environment.

25.   However, in the depth of itself, the spiritual world suffers.

26.   But all that is not matter is elusive to it, the truth cannot be proved by experience.

27.   It is therefore disgusted by the inadequacy of matter, desolated by the vanity of the Ideal. Nothingness of life and nothingness of dream.

28.   Then it sinks into the abyss of the Ideal, despising matter and gets lost in the dream, but the consciousness of its nobility does not gives its empty visions the beauty of life, nor does it give security to its hope.

29.   Or, recognizing that it can neither affirm the invisible world nor deny it, it is content to know matter, and to do its duty without seeking if it is a divine depth from which emanates in its thoughts the love of Good.

30.   Or, also rejecting duty without belief, the last incarnation, diminished, sad, and the most sublime of its spiritual greatness;

31.   It then no longer thinks itself to be a bubble of the River.

32.   But sometimes, although it does not act on the visible without the body, a feeling is revived in it of its strength.

33.   It remembers that it is a cause and thinks that, delivered from the flesh, perhaps, it would see God.

34.   But how to be free from the body without dying? And God forbids to die voluntarily. Ecstasy delivers like death, says the Initiate.

35.   Then the Soul absorbs itself into this science that learns to die without leaving the earth, and makes the body a garment that can always be worn after having divested it.

36.   It flies in the Aour[15]. It drinks the blood of God and bathes in it.

37.   Then it gathers in the Unity of the Dark Absolute.

38.   Penetrating directly and by himself all forms of being, universal science becomes easy and identical to his thought.

39.   The ebb and flow of life, the immense force that intoxicates and drives mad, it sees them from above; it ascends to the summit of the Towers, whose shadow falls on the upper sea.

40.   The souls of the dead, the vanished centuries, the vanished truths, are for them living, actual, recovered.

---

[15] A.B.: Hebrew אור, light

41.   It knows the bodies and the Spirits from within, as though it becomes their cause.

42.   And radiates itself in the innumerable immensity until it regains consciousness of infinitude.

GEBURAH

I. Passion and Fate

1.   Passion, when science does not compel it to pull the Good, - as the chariots of the symbolic gods are dragged by panthers and tigresses - tears that which flatters it and then tears itself.

2.   Nature, destined to destroy to renew itself, attracts man to death by the trap of desire.

3.   But all these monsters who devour the weak and impure spirit are none the less the necessary agents of salvation.

4.   You will not reach Heaven if you are not carried on the back of Satan.

5.   Evil is an excess or a corruption of force in nature and instinct in the soul. This excess - tamed - can become omnipotence, and this corruption, -understood in its cause-, holiness.

6.   For the Almighty is equilibrium, but equilibrium in the Absolute which is excess, since it is supreme.

7.   The corruption of the instincts is due to a contempt for their insufficiency which would leave the vice for ecstasy, if he knew his own nature well.

8.   And the corruption of the forces discovers in the decomposition of the spiritual fluids which it delivers and which serve to the Initiate as weapons against the matter.

9.   Make Lightning work for Elohim. Sculpt a temple to God, in the granite, with strikes of thunder, and you will not risk being struck down by lightning.

10.   All calamity, all collapse: Passion or Fate.

11.   What is passion? A blind love always uncertain of the value of that which he possesses.

12.   What is fate? The sequence of Principles and Consequences, insofar as it is not planned and one cannot modify or evade his action.

13.   Passion, ignorant energy; fate, force ignored; passion and fate, ignorance.

14.   Seek in love only the possession of the Divine, have no other feelings than those which can last forever, transfigure passion into charity.

15. Is it necessary to annihilate human love in oneself? No; but it is necessary to attach oneself only to the noble souls and to recognize them by the discernment of the spirits.

16. The smallest events to come, the most subtle consequences, not only are inscribed in advance in the light, but obey the Numbers.

17. Occult science is no less profound than fate, but it is higher.

18. The supreme initiation detaches so completely from matter that the soul no longer even needs to foresee fate to triumph over it. Destiny and misfortune become foreign to it; it watches them pass by.

19. Death for man: The most visible and the most terrible mystery. In his hands: The supreme empire. To understand death, unparalleled intuition of intelligence.

20. Whoever dies and is reborn at will, will know that which he desires.

21. Whoever kills and resurrects at will, will do whatever he desires.

22. To die is to live, to a higher degree, an existence analogous to that which is abandoned and more subtle.

23. This existence must subsequently lead to a lower incarnation than that which was left, to a higher one or to emancipation.

24. No one has the right of life and death with impunity but the man who is without passion or hatred and who does not avenge himself.

25. If, by Black magic, a cursed man acquires this power, sooner or later he will lose it, and his torment will be no less incredible than his usurpation.

26. Thus the privilege of the true Mage consists in the eternity of his victory.

27. Momentary victory, evil makes its diadem, as if it were wrapping to his forehead the clouds of the West which are extinguished.

II.   Intuition and Calculation

1.   The instinctive divination of analogies and the algebraic registration of laws that move the world, the mind[16] has no other ways of knowing.

2.   Isolated, the prophetic instinct intermingled with errors, its miraculous discoveries and mathematical uncertainty never exceeds the average order of certainties.

3.   It is to the broad views of divination that we owe the attempts of synthesis and, without inspiration, the fragmentary and positive science would have progressed poorly.

4.   The Infinite, clairvoyance hovers there. But the dark Absolute, science alone creates the abstract conception that allows the soul to recognize reality when it reaches it.

5.   Election begins with desire, with a vague call to the Archangels, but the Initiate only attains by Reason and Numbers.

6.   Charity, mother of the Saint, gives birth to intuition, the Will, mother of the Magus, calculation.

---

[16] A.B.: in French, "esprit" can mean mind, spirit, intelligence, etc.

7.   Pure intuitives have prevailed. Success often belongs to them more than to thinkers. But a force that endures, outside of science, there is none.

8.   We must remain impartial and fair, and not listen to our personal wishes when we aim for lucidity. We must learn to say: anything that is not proven remains as nothing, and to sacrifice the joy of the soul for a long time when we aspire for certainty.

9.   Without intuition, thought dies and dries out like flesh from which blood has fled. Without the cold Kabbalah, it deforms like flesh from which the bone has been removed.

10.   Clairvoyance leads to death, when one does not submit it to the central and fixed truth. And dreams to ruin when they rebel against the Arcana.

11.   Occultism seems like an extravagance, a mysticism. It is Temperance, Prudence, Balance.

12.   Almighty because it neglects no effect, no cause, and embraces the entire being, without illusion or bias, it is obliged to silence. The universality subverts incomplete reason.

13.   Much better than temperament, the mind is transformed to the point that its past nature cannot understand it or well-nigh remember it.

14.   One can impart infallible premonitions just as easily as false views.

15.   The science of the Prophets consists in the marriage of male reason and female imagination, of male will and female enthusiasm.

16.   War exists only through ignorance. Even the unjust would come to his ends without shedding blood or hurting opinion, if he knew.

17.   To overcome powerful weapons rather than many. Two empires, one inferior in population but maintained concentrated in a single territory, the other populous, but formed of provinces separated from each other by other nations; sooner or later, the first will bring down the second.

18.   Certain intelligences, understanding all but existing only outside of themselves, are astonished at their defeat during the admiration of their resources. They forget that character more so than knowledge wins the victory. Having never penetrated them, they will not reach the cause of their adversities.

19.   Intellectual initiative is developed by imagination, moderated by instinct and balanced by Reason.

20.   Love is no longer wrong to substitute illusions for what is, when it conquers the strength to transfigure what is in what it loves.

21.   All power not identical to the one who exercises it, perishes.

22.   The teaching to man of the Absolute by the blossoming and the destruction of the forms which represent the various attributes of the Absolute: Purpose of the world.

23.   The Sphinx lying upon the summit of the heavens on the last terrace of the Empyrean, observes passion and the desire to create and kill, below him, the stars and their Humanities. All that passion and desire live blindly, the Sphinx knows the Law, the truth, the logic and that which it proves, he who seems dead and immobile, it is the infinitude of the pains and drunkenness possible to their highest degree of consciousness, concentration and intensity.

III.   Perfections

1.   The absolute Being, God, exceeds in perfection all that man knows by science or by dream. But divine perfection separates itself from all known perfections, not because it differs from them to the point of being devoid of it, but because it reunites them to their purity, light and power supreme, incomprehensible.

2.   It is not, therefore, ignorance, nor to reject from his heart nature and man by ambition of a mutilated and negative holiness which elevates to God, but the love and science of all men and universal creation.

3.   All the orders of realities, from the infernal world to the divine world, if compared to God and absolute perfection, they appear incomplete, inert or corrupt, they are none the less irreproachable and perfect in themselves.

4.   They are each the exact consequence and the development (beautiful for the contemplation of he who has the sentiment of science and the law) by which special interior causes, apparent, spontaneous, determined, are manifested. By this they are perfect and cannot be conceived different from what they are.

5.   The pure and ignorant soul is astonished at crimes. But what is monstrous in man is natural to the tiger.

6.   Instead of studying the criminal by considering him as a man, a term in which we embody a collective idea of human nature which is an abstraction, it is necessary to study him as a solitary being, to examine why and to what degree he approaches or is distinguished from an animal by brutishness or conscious perversity.

7.   You will understand by a meditation of this nature that evil, in a certain point of view, is a perfection.

8.   And you will glorify the Eternal and his thought when you have admired the precise and marvelous action which creates by a succession of equally beautiful evolutions, the soul of the righteous or the cruelest of egoists.

9.   But for that you shall not tolerate evil in you, nor around you.

10.   It is the universality of the justice of God, and the beauty of the laws of matter and of the spirit which are admirable in a wicked person. But if he is not a fool, a beast or possessed, the same justice that gives him the perfection of evil, intends this evil to degrade and torture him.

11.   Do not punish, do not kill. Separate the demon-man from the people of God, then allow his soul to act. The punishment of the perverse is perverse itself.

12.   Thus the world is an indefinite flowering of relative perfections emanating from an absolute and infinite perfection. These perfections form a regular hierarchy whose summit touches the Absolute and whose base stretches out from it, in the Darkness.

TIPHERETH

I.   The Science of Christ

1.   In principio erat Verbum et Verbum erat apud Deum et Deus erat Verbum.[17]

2.   All that creation abandons in the eyes, God is in principle, and he is in fullness.

3.   Humanity-God, prior to Humanity, is Christ. Nature-God, prior to nature, is the Holy Spirit.

4.   The Father has no grand analogy.

5.   The correspondences created of the divine persons present the image of the works of Christ and of the Holy Spirit, but analogous support to them, not identical.

6.   The consubstantial Word corresponds to the emanation of souls, sacrificed to their trials, risen to their salvation. But the Word is not Humanity, Man is not the Son of God.

---

[17] A.B.: Gospel of John 1:1

7.   The Holy Spirit corresponds by its gifts to the forces of nature.

8.   But it is not these forces, it directs them.

9.   The solitary Soul, earthly Humanity and universal Humanity, all three find the symbol of their birth in the Word, of their trials in the sorrowful Christ, of their deliverance in the glorious Christ.

10.   Initiatic Wisdom, Corner Stone of the Temple of Science, is in faithful analogy with Christ, Corner Stone of the Celestial Temple.

11.   The solitary soul is fallen from the Aour Ha Ensoph, it has lost Eden where it was shaded by giant trees whose branches bloom in stars;

12.   Like Jesus, from the heart of his Father fell into a body of suffering.

13.   By death alone, or Initiation, which is an inner death, the Soul can return to Paradise, like Christ after the sepulcher.

14.   Absolute holiness only shines in the Magi, and absolute Initiation is only luminous in the splendor of the saints.

15.   To become a saint, it is not enough to know that God exists; it is necessary to understand the mystery of the Holy Trinity, as far as that is possible to man.

16.   And to thus see the formidable form of Yod-Héva vanish.

17.   And the God of charity appear beyond eternal vengeance.

18.   It is not enough to become a Mage to know that the Great Arcanum exists.

19.   One must alter one by one the three principles of nature until the shadow and the brutal thickness which conceals them goes up in smoke.

20.   But the whole Gospel is nothing but initiation.

21.   And the History of terrestrial Humanity also shows a golden age, a fall and long pains, then the Empire of the Messiah.

22.   And the History of Eternity after the creation of the worlds tells of their corruption and their slow trials, and ends with the prophecy of their salvation.

II.   Initiation and the Gospel

1.   To be born of a Virgin was the privilege of the Man-God. To be spiritually reborn from a symbolic Virgin is the beginning of the Nuctemeron[18] for the Adepts.

2.   Mary, freshness of the sea, lily of the waters, grace of the evening, voice of consolation in the twilight. In your thought, I have sheltered my most distant hope as in an immovable ivory tower on the shores of the Empyrean, beyond the Heavens ...

3.   The symbolic Virgin who gives birth to a divine Son is for the Magi, grace in the metaphysical world, the occult truth in the intellectual world, the Aour in the natural world.

4.   The grace of God, the breath of wisdom, Ruach Chokmael, unique influence from above that cannot mislead the soul that receives it.

5.   The occult Truth, the only doctrine that has not been defiled by men, because they have not known it.

---

[18] A.B.: Nuctemeron: The twelve hours of Apollonius of tyana

6.   The Aour, the only natural force that has remained indomitable to the profane, and which at once replaces and controls all the other forces of Nature.

7.   When God has given birth in your soul to the son of the Virgin, the new man who is yourself and more than you, because in him is incarnated the thought of God that emanated you, the shepherds and the Magi will adore him.

8.   May the instincts of your heart and of your faith be prostrated at the feet of your Ideal.

9.   And may the royal sciences also recognize the divinity of your Desire.

10.   For, without the divine and interior spirit, instincts will be heavy and the sciences will mislead you.

11.   Then you will be baptized by John the Baptist, that is to say that the Angels, who are future men and as precursors of the Magi will bathe you in the Jordan, in the invisible river where the soul is sanctified, where the body is glorified.

12.   And Satan will come to tempt you, for as soon as the Soul pulls on its chain, it stretches itself, and if the Soul does not have the strength to break it, it falls again, defeated by the effort, into a worse slavery.

13.   And Satan will say to you: Affirm your new power with wonders. And he will offer you the Empire of the world.

14.   But, like Christ, answer him with words of humility and renunciation. The empire will be eternal for the one who disdains to reign.

15.   And you shall serve your scepter of the Initiate only to heal the sick, to raise the dead, to heal the guilty also and to resurrect the great sinners.

16.   And nothing will show from your science and your reign except your goodness and the simplicity of your life.

17.   As long as the LORD will not order you to manifest your works, you will fulfill them in the mystery, you will not make known to you those whom you will save.

18.   What would God be in the world if the men he inspires throw to the pigs what they receive from him? The external cults mask God, the scholars of matter deny or ignore him.

19.   But the blindness of the cults, the carelessness or the hatred of the scholars does not acquire for them the supreme Arcana of the Occult. A glory remains innaccessible of which we are the guardians.

20.   The majesty of the Lord is inviolable in this world only by the darkness of our silence.

21.   Rarely, for the great progress of the earth, the Lord commands the Initiate to perform miracles in the eyes of all.

22.   But he does not need to reveal the dogmas and rites that make theurgy possible.

23.   God willing, you will not hide your works, but you will always be silent about the Quaternary generation.

24.   Ask, and it shall be given you; seek, and ye shall find; knock, and it shall be opened unto you.[19]

25.   Beyond duty is devotion; beyond science, ecstasy; beyond work, the miracle. But duty exists by devotion, ecstasy by science and the miracle by the work.

26.   Enter through the narrow gate, because the wide gate and the spacious path lead to death.

27.   You only have need of one Master, the Lord, of one truth, the grand Arcanum, and of one weapon, prayer.

---

[19] A.B.: Matthew 7:7

28.   Seek first the Kingdom of God and His righteousness[20]. The universal science will be given to you in addition.

29.   You will walk on the sea where the stars sway - and which surges in waves on the stars.

30.   When you become the tabernacle of the living God, your light will spread to the four cardinal points of the Intelligence and illuminate the twelve virtues that are the twelve apostles of Neshamah, the human Word.

31.   Your face will be like the sun, your clothes like snow, Moses will teach you the past, Elijah will uncover the future.

32.   But all this is only the first work.

33.   You must die, remain in the tomb for three days, and resurrect to sit at the right hand of God.

34.   You will be crucified at the center of the Cross, in the midst of the four elements, and you will lie in the occult tomb, and after three operations that are signified by the three days, you will return to our Heavenly Father to rest in the great peace of the heart.

---

[20] A.B.: Justice

III. <u>Regeneration</u>

1.   In the work of the Sages it is necessary to add to the elusive ether a Tangible, fixed body of the same nature as the ether and to unite them into a single compound.

2.   In the work of salvation, the flesh must be joined to the Son of God.

3.   Divinity, so as not to cause death, coldness, and selfishness, must become human before approaching Man.

4.   But that is not by taking on the vices, the meanness, and the superstitious ugliness of the Earth.

5.   It is to our nature free from sin, as pure as its creation, but pure by will and not by ignorance, that God is confounded to reveal himself to us without rendering us inhuman.

6.   He who does not know how to love and to have the Absolute in his brothers as one perfection results in damnation.

7.   The desire of the infinite, when it inspires the indifference to live by the heart, does not bring forth the Saints, but the Demons of genius[21].

8.   Until the day of his fall the Antichrist will be triumphant and vulgarly fortunate and the Christ suffered until his resurrection.

9.   But the Antichrist falls for eternity, and the Christ resurrects for eternity.

10.   There is no great work, those of the Sages among all, which does not have abnegation and pain for its duration.

11.   We do not reach true power by immediate victory, true love by pleasure, true science by the nonchalant contemplation of forms.

12.   Torture matter, by analysis you will know, test your will by the contempt of the conquests that God does not esteem, you will be King forever, torment your soul with the dream of moral perfection and the religion of fidelity, you will love.

---

[21] A.B.: one definition of genie in French is "an imaginary being, good or bad"; it can also be a spirit, among other translations.

13. You will notice that the time of trials and putrefaction, forty days, is marked by a number often found in Scripture.

14. For God's people wandered forty years in the desert before reaching the Promised Land.

15. Moses remained forty days on Sinai, Elijah took refuge for forty days in solitude, and Jesus Christ fasted for forty days in the desert where Satan came to tempt him.

16. He spoke on the earth for forty months, he slept in the sepulcher forty hours; Forty days elapsed between the Resurrection and the Ascension, and forty years after the Ascension, Jerusalem was overthrown by the Romans.

17. The secret body of the Magi for the profane seems vulgar, ugly, loaded with miseries and evils, as Jesus appeared to his persecutors. But he who has the intelligence comprised of Cesar or of Christ would be master of the Future.

18. And he who has the intelligence can divine which, the sun of the Sages or of the sun of men, illuminates realities.

19. Jesus, from the stable, carried in him the victory which, at his second advent, he will give man and the world, as the first advent he gave the dream and the faith.

20.   And the Magus as soon as he sees the occult sun conquers the universal science and possesses it in power.

21.   The secret body of the Sages must be inundated with the perspiration of blood as Christ was inundated in the Garden of Olives and lose all strength as Christ was discouraged[22] and felt his sorrowful soul until death.

22.   But, revived by the unknown fire, this secret body accepts and then supports the tortures which lead it to the sepulcher, then to the Resurrection and Triumph.

23.   Neither the senses, nor the instruments that man has invented to multiply or prolong them, nor reason knows the being in its truth.

24.   Human Science like the visible world are both symbols of the hidden nature and the inaccessible God.

25.   All the human sciences, useful to the flesh and the earth by their applications, and beneficent to the mind by the habituation of thinking with precision that they impose upon it, serve no purpose on the day of death or after death.

---

[22] A.B.: in French découragé means to lose courage and can be translated as discouraged, despondent, dispirited, depressed, downhearted, etc.

26.   That alone is worthy of conquest that death does not change.

27.   When you are lying in agony, it is there that you will know the price of things. It is in agony that you have to see yourself in imagination before choosing your path and doing your work.

28.   Do not begin as the profane do by scattering yourself in nature such as your eyes see it nor in the passions, as your instincts understand them.

29.   But first, ask yourself if man is an exact instrument of knowledge.

30.   What does it matter that you have seen many things and that you have kept them if your eyes lie? And what does the science of appearances matter if it varies with the organs?

31.   The constant connections that you notice between two illusions at the price of the science that these illusions are veiling you are the same!

32.   The doctrine of the Magi teaches how to regenerate the body and spirit of man, until they contemplate the being such as it is.

33.   The doctrine of the profane teaches to develop the body and mind of man in its earthly imperfection and to know the being as it appears.

34.   By charity and virtue the soul and the body are purified and by miracles they are transfigured.

35.   Religion, in its commandments, reveals charity and virtue and, in its symbolic legends, the Arcana that the Hierophant-King makes burst into miracles.

Humanity

NETZACH

I.　The Mystery of the Will of God

1.　Here we are: In the last days man will descend to the depths of matter, into the caves of destiny, and ascend to the highest of justice in the abyss of intelligence.

2.　He will descend to the depths of destiny, and he will learn why he is born of woman and why he must be reborn from death.

3.　And why God seals him in the womb, and seals him in the tomb.

4.　God will say: I have desired your perfection and your divinity rather than your happiness, for happiness without nobility is degradation and as long as perfection is not reached the nobility is forbidden.

5.　The perfection which is not given to the soul by the soul is inferior: I created you free.

6.   After your birth in heaven, I have tested[23] you.

7.   I had created you free to the point where you could give up, if not the indestructible principle, at least the action of your freedom, so free that you could want to be a slave.

8.   You have been delivered unto evil, tempted to know it and do not yet understand that you do not know it, even as you do it.

9.   Because to do it one must love it, and to love it by ignoring the intimate nothingness.

10.   So you have fallen into the matter, and you must go through the cycle of the revolution of souls and begin your successive lives again as long as you do not do the Good by yourself.

11.   You have fallen to the point that you are unhappy, helpless, ignorant. You must reconquer happiness, royalty, science.

12.   But if you reconquer happiness without charity, royalty without devotion, science without prayer, I will take it

------

[23] A.B.: éprouver – proven, tried, tested. Can also mean to feel or experience.

away from you, and I will cast you back into slavery and bestiality.

13.   And I cause you to die, and to live again, soul and body, works and thoughts, millions and millions of times until you love God and men with a selfless, heroic love.

14.   You see that it is foolish to seek in voluntary death a refuge against the harshness of duty, despair or remorse in suicide only leads to another existence and more bitter than it would have been without it, for it renders more cruel, as every crime, the future incarnation of he who commits it.

15.   I do not receive you in me until you become like me, when you are just and martyred by yourself.

16.   Your choice is an effect of my grace in that in creating you I have created the principle of all your acts. But your very choice, isolated is your work, your work alone.

17.   When you have preferred virtue, then my grace comes to your aid, but the initial preference I cannot have for you, you must have it.

18.   All that I give you of truth and glory, you once possessed in Paradise, but you only possessed it by me and you recover it by your merits.

19.   The errors of men, their maledictions against pain and destiny, come from their lack of esteem for their soul and their lack of courage to struggle against nature in order to free themselves from it and to tame it.

20.   If they dare to think themselves noble enough to desire to be perfect and make themselves so, my Shekinah will come down upon them, they will see me without dying.

21.   I fully protect only those who have begun to love me and to live in a holy manner without my help.

II.   Justice

1.   The highest degree of love is to create the happiness of those whom one loves. There is no true happiness beyond the will to do good. To do Good is to fulfill Justice. The highest degree of love is the practice, the example and the apostolate of Justice.

2.   Pity and rigor are also incomplete.

3.   To desire the perfection of beings and your own, to work to create this perfection, is to practice true Justice.

4. True justice does not consist precisely in the equality of merits and rewards, but in their equivalence.

5. The connection of merits to their sanctions is the condition and the means, not the principle of Justice. It is the Love of the perfection of beings which is this Principle:

6. The rigorous and symmetrical equality of merits and rewards would not satisfy as their equivalence.

7. Often we do not obtain through our efforts what seems to be their direct consequence, and the Holy Spirit directs us through them, not to what we have desired, but to what is most favorable to our salvation.

8. To desire the Perfection of Souls leads God to sometimes send to the Righteous unmerited pains, which are necessary for their moral progress, and not to punish the wicked when this punishment cannot aid in their redemption.

9. Justice is for man to think and to do in all orders of acts or thoughts manifested or interior, which will make others and himself the most like God.

III. Authority

1.   The Lord commands man to choose the Good in perfect freedom, to establish a law which compels human societies to the practice of the Good, seems contradictory to the order of the Eternal.

2.   It is not so: The exterior practice of Justice is all that the Law can obtain, and God does not worry about this exterior practice and judges only from hidden feelings.

3.   If evil attracts, by the seduction of lust and revolt, the Good corrupts by the desire to deceive it, to turn it hypocritically to serve the passions and also by the pride and the contempt of the charity that inspires the cold spirits their maleficent and hard virtue.

4.   A good Soul only returns to Paradise after having overcome the temptations of Heaven as well as the temptations of Hell.

5.   An evil soul is rejected only after having lived among the Righteous, having suffered evil and persevered, in spite of good example and punishment, in its baseness.

6.   Good, evil, and their opposing forces fight in nature and humanity. God contemplates the battle and allows the

Souls to traverse all the hells, all the lands, all the suns, tempted to lose themselves by Evil or by Good.

7.   So do not be afraid to oppose the will of Elohim by a perfect law on the earth. When a world changes in nature, the immensity still contains innumerable worlds analogous to that which it was originally.

8.   But the Messianic Kingdom will not be for the weak and impure heart or cruel and stingy any less dangerous than the dead or dying societies.

9.   Prophet of Yod-Hêva, the earth will answer to my call by the prediction of our defeat our by doubt.

10.   For me, what I predict is our victory. Now your time has come, Initiates of the mysteries of the God of the Magi.

11.   Let us rise, then, to prepare and establish in the world the omnipotence of the eternal religion, the dominion of the absolute science, the reign of the ideal beauty, and the universal Empire of the Messiah.

HOD

I.   The Church

1.   You will love God with a divine love.

2.   You will love God as his Son loves him.

3.   And you will make your soul worthy of this feeling.

4.   You will offer to God the homage of ceremonies and prayer.

5.   But you will learn from the Magi the meaning of the ceremonies and the meaning of the prayers so that the inner light may be present in the images and the words.

6.   And you will follow the words and rites of the Church of Christ.

7.   After the second Advent of the Messiah we will recite the ancient prayer and the ancient symbol in memory of the sacrifice.

8.   But we will recite the Messianic Prayer and the messianic symbol in glorification of victory.

9.   And they will make the sign of the cross to clothe themselves and to be penetrated by the Eternal.

10.   But the Quaternary invocation will be made by raising the right hand and pronouncing the name YodHeVavHe, face turned to the East.

11.   To impose on creatures, by the will of man, the will of God.

II.   <u>Marriage</u>

1.   Among those who will consecrate themselves to the service of the Lord, those who are not destined to clairvoyance, will live in a state of marriage.

2.   He must live the human life or attain to a real superior existence. If one renounces the acts of Humanity without doing the acts of the archangel, then the body and the intelligence will atrophy or hypocritical vices will eat away at the flesh and the mind.

3.   In secular society those whom God does not call to clairvoyance will have to marry as well.

4.   Souls are born through couples. The absolute Love unites Soul-Sisters as they find each other again.

5.   In your youth you will look for the sister of your soul and if you are worthy that God hears you, you will find her.

6.   But it is rare for the two souls born of the same ecstasy of God to descend on the earth at the same time. Often one suffers in one world and the other in another.

7.   The principle of ideal and infinite love is the original unity of two souls.

8.   But this unity is not the only principle of love on earth.

9.   In Paradise there is no more birth or death, and love has no point but to complete a soul of man by a woman's soul because God is only fully understood and adored by a couple.

10.   But on earth, love is above all for the preservation of the human race.

11.   It is by the birth of children that Souls who have fallen into the kingdom of darkness or into the elemental spheres are reincarnated.

12.   It is through the birth of children that descend into the world, those who have fallen from the sublimes ethers for a necessary trial which they come to undergo, or the increase of their sins.

13.   Thus not only does the birth perpetuate the human race and keep woman stronger than death, but it is the way of the elemental spirits ascension to Humanity and the descent to Humanity of the celestial spirits.

14.   Every man therefore has the duty to marry to have children unless he is an Initiate.

15.   For the Initiate, through invisible miracles and prayers, ascends directly from Hell to Heaven and descends down directly from Heaven to Hell the Souls who undergo their revolution without passing through the earth.

16.   You shall marry even if you do not find the soul sister, because your duty is to give back to the spirits who want to come into the world what your parents did for you when you wanted to come into the world.

17.   But if you do not meet the Soul-sister, you will only marry for material views and self-interest.

18.   You will look for a woman such that if you do not love her with Absolute Love at least you will love her with a love that is in promise and prepares you to deserve her.

III.   <u>Vocations</u>

1.   The principle of property is analogous to the principle of differentiation of Spirits.

2.   Each spirit has received a vocation from the Eternal, and if two Magi attain the Absolute identically through science, they will remain different by a personal genius which will determine them in the choice of their works.

3.   All that can belong to men - thought or matter - is the field of work, and must be shared between men according to their vocation.

4.   A property is a function, an obligation to a duty. Whosoever fulfills the duty, that he keeps the property and does not fulfill it, it shall be taken from him, so saith the Absolute.

5.   But the Absolute does not reign alone, no more in the exploitation of the Earth than in marriage. The collective

unity of the worlds where one dies is the family and not the person.

6.   To annihilate the inheritance would be to destroy the cause of passionate and broad-minded labor in all men who have no genius.

7.   The thirst for survival in the child is the immortality of the flesh.

8.   We must reconcile family and justice.

9.   At the death of a man, if his heir is capable of his function, it will be preserved to him.

10.   If he is incapable of doing so but shows himself worthy of an equivalent function, the first will be withdrawn in exchange for the second.

11.   If he is completely incapable, he will be left with enough to subsist, but the rest of the fortune will be dedicated by the Magi to charity.

12.   So that even to an invalid man the labor of his Fathers will not have been made in vain.

13.   But justice will no longer be forgotten.

14.   The science of the Magi allows them to discern the predestination of children and elevate them in their vocation.

15.   Crimes will be foretold from childhood through occult wisdom, for in sleep the soul is kneaded like wax by the will of the Magus who has put him to sleep.

16.   Free will is not violated by this suppression of crimes.

17.   Because, in the long run, the Soul arrives, in the successive existences, to not be able to undergo any more influences.

18.   Impose good ones on it as long as it receives them. Otherwise it will always receive, but bad.

19.   Once imperturbable, it will freely choose good or bad.

20.   If there are imperturbable criminals who do not master the Art of the seers, they will be reduced to impotence, but one does not kill in the Kingdom of God.

YESOD

I.   The Magi

1.   In the Days of the Messiah, the World will be ruled by the Son of God and the great Church of the Magi. The Redeemer will be the Supreme Prophet, the Sovereign Pontiff and the King of Kings.

2.   Master of the Prophets, he will have on his left a Pontiff who will be the chief of the Priests and on his right a Hero who will be the chief of the warriors.

3.   For the great Church of the Magi will be comprised of Prophets, priests and warriors.

4.   The Prophets will be devoted to the study of the divine sciences and the practice of miracles.

5.   Priests to the worship of the Lord, to the instruction of the faithful.

6.   Warriors to the administration and defense of the Kingdom of God.

7. And all government will belong to these three orders;

8. By the Word.

9. It is the Ternary that moves the universal being. But there are several ternaries. One is like Tiphereth above Yesod and Yesod above Malkuth.

10. The other like Kether in the middle of Binah and Chokmah.

11. The second ternary is that of the organization of Power; the other merely expresses the natural distribution of Intelligences as superior, middle, inferior.

12. But if the superiors govern the lower ones by the middle, among the superiors as among all there are the central Souls of the right and those of left.

13. And those on the right and on the left must obey the first so that there is unity in the power.

14. The Priests represent the Authority, the tradition, the tempering force, which resists, delays and gives stability.

15. The warriors represent the progress, the action, the force that attacks, renews, advances and gives energy.

16.   But the Prophets represent the divine truth and the divine will which govern both the forces of resistance and movement and correct them one by the other. The Absolute is not only the summit but the center of the summit.

17.   The Prophets will prevent the Priests from atrophying Intelligence by tradition.

18.   They will prevent the warriors from destroying the Tradition by innovations that are errors.

19.   They will harmonize the geniuses that conserve with the geniuses that create.

20.   Warriors will have power only for the defense and the political and social administration of the Kingdom and to render Justice.

21.   Priests will have power only for the teaching of the truth and for the religious administration of the Kingdom and to give the faithful the sacraments.

22.   The Prophets will have all the rights of the other two orders, but will not exercise them unless the other two orders fail.

23.   The warriors will make the political and social laws, and the priests the religious rules.

24.   But nothing will have the force of law that has not been approved by the Prophets, and what the Prophets reject will be abolished.

II.   The Election

1.   The Priests, Warriors and Prophets will be elected by Initiation.

2.   From childhood the Elect to whom the Magi have recognized a destiny of Prophet, Priest or Warrior will be raised differently from other men.

3.   Election to the rank of Priest, Warrior or Prophet will not be given by heredity, suffrage, fate, or anything other than trials, the series of which will begin with life.

4.   And if before electing or increasing in rank a Mage of such or such order, he will undergo a solemn ordeal.

5.   One will not be judged by the success of this test alone, but by all previous trials and by all that is known of the soul, character and actions of the Recipient.

6.   At his reception, if the Mage is to be a warrior, he will be asked for profound knowledge of the Arcana of the World of Assiah and the verbal and summary science of the Arcana of Yetzirah and of Briah and his faith in Atziluth.

7.   If he is to be a priest, he will be asked for a profound knowledge of the Arcana of Yetzirah and Briah and the verbal and summary knowledge of Atziluth and of Assiah.

8.   But if he is to be a Prophet, he will be asked for the absolute science and the practice of the Arcana of Assiah, Yetzirah, Briah, and Atziluth.

9.   A priest upon completing his initiation may become a Prophet. A Warrior may, under the same conditions, become a Prophet. But a Warrior cannot become a Priest, nor a Priest become a Warrior.

10.   Each of the orders will be divided into three great classes, according to the degree of wisdom and virtue.

11.   Each of the three great classes will have its chief. That of the highest class of Priests will be Sovereign Pontiff, that of the highest class of Warriors will be their Prince and that of the highest class of the Prophets will be Grand-Hierophant. But above the Grand-Hierophant will reign over

the Three Orders and the Earth, the Redeemer, the Son of God, the Messiah.

III. <u>Men</u>

1.	There will be only one flock and one shepherd.

2.	All the earth will be one immense empire.

3.	The human races will develop in peace, according to their various geniuses, towards Holiness, Intelligence, Beauty and Happiness.

4.	The Warriors will contain the wicked. But there will be no war between the peoples.

5.	The impurity of love will be disdained. The couples will unite as in ecstasy.

6.	Life will be beautiful and radiant with angels.

7.	And even those who are not Initiates will have visions, and immortality will be certainty.

8.	And Humanity will be calm and indefatigable like the earth.

9. The prophets with their voices will bring down the influence of the Cherubs.

10. And the blessings of Yod-héva, Elohim.

11. The strength of God will enter the flesh.

12. Disease will pass.

13. Death will sing.

14. And everything will rise in harmony, because in descending we find the struggle and by the ascent the soul attains peace.

15. Michael will lead Satan and Satan will stretch his arms to the chains to atone.

16. The sea will enter the Palace of the Antichrist, half collapsed at the edge of the waves, and will resound under the vaults of porphyry to the praise of the Eternal.

17. Spirits will unite the earth with distant suns.

18. The ether, in its flight, will illuminate like a field covered with dew.

19. The desires of the Nations will be revealed to the Magi.

20. And any just request will be granted.

21. And such, in the last days, will be fulfilled the faith of Abraham, the great dream of Moses, the prediction of David.

22. And the hope of God.

Prophecy

MALKUTH

I.   The Judgment of the Earth

1.   Here are the times to come. Here are the heavens rolling towards the earth.

2.   The occult Sun will engulf the world; the flame of heaven will shake the earth in its smoking jaws.

3.   Death descends on your paths whistling and turns its scythe like a sling.

4.   The earth is black, it looks like bones burned by fire.

5.   The slain fall by large armies.

6.   The nations are overthrown like mountains that fall down.

7.   The material heavens are shattered by the wind; they hang like broken doors with hinges that are coming unsealed.

8.   And the spiritual heavens descend,

9.   Like sacred, immense animals, each of which shades its wings one of the four parts of the ether.

10.   The Eagle passes like a swirl of snow and the Antichrist is lacerated in the aquilon[24].

11.   The lion tears the flanks of the earth with his nails and the tatters of continents, laden with peoples, fall below the earth in the night.

12.   The Divine Man contemplates the ruins with eyes of vengeance.

13.   And Taurus rushes into the depths of Gehenna crushing the damned who have just fallen by the millions and whose groans rise in vain to the deserted land and prolong in solitude.

---

[24] A.B.: aquilon = northern wind

II.   The Kingdom of the millennium

1.   Serenity of the days of the Messiah ... Ancient pains fly away to the heavens in the steam of prayers and falling on the mountains and in the plains in rains of delights and great rivers of magnificence ...

2.   On the earth, purified by the flame, the heat of the heart of God will swell the harvest, the blood of God will flow in the wine.

3.   Men will walk intoxicated in the moving soul of the Eternal.

4.   Clusters of giant roses hang from the walls of Jerusalem and tall lilies like towers will flourish in the light above the Temple.

5.   The Messiah will appear on the threshold of the Temple, his eyes full of the eternity of Judgment.

6.   On the five continents and on the five oceans of the world in the seas and on the islands, the Son of God will be King and Pontiff for centuries.

7.   Like a Queen coming out of the dark waters of the cave, whose black tiara is gird by iron and encrusted with sapphires.

8.   Humanity has come to the Redeemer.

9.   And the Solar King, whose dreams are firmaments and the words of the stars, has embraced the dark Queen so that she conceived the new Man.

10.   And they will be united for a thousand years.

11.   Their love will veil their foreheads with noble thoughts and their body of perfumes floating on their limbs like clouds.

12.   At that time it will no longer be the sign of the cross that will be the sign of Christ, but the star with five rays, the star of Triumph.

13.   And when the thousand years are over, the Messiah will leave the Earth and evil men will be born and the Earth will be destroyed.

III. The Last Judgment

1.   At the Last Judgment creation will return to nothingness.

2.   And there will be nothing but Hell and Heaven.

3.   Those who loved will be the heat of Heaven.

4.   And those who have suffered for their Love will be like a fire of glory in the Empyrean.

5.   And hell will close on the hateful souls.

6.   But damnation will be eternal only for those who will eternally refuse to love.

7.   There will be no more matter, there will be no more Angels, nor Man in Paradise: all souls there will be perfect.

8.   The forms will only exist in the Light as reflections of the thoughts of the creatures and meditations of the Lord.

9.   And nothing will live any more than the Souls in the universal Charity of God,

10.   And God in the love and incorruptible freedom of the Souls. Alleluia.

Made in United States
North Haven, CT
10 January 2023

30903711R00071